GEORGE WASHINGTON
Country Boy, Country Gentleman

written by Tracey E. Dils

For Phillip, my little gentleman

illustrated by Dick Smolinski

Published by Worthington Press
10100 SBF Drive, Pinellas Park, Florida 34666

Copyright © 1992 by Worthington Press

All rights reserved. No portion of this book may be reproduced, stored in a retrieval system, or transmitted, in any form or by any means, electronic, mechanical, photocopying, recording or otherwise without prior written permission from the publisher.

Printed in the United States of America

2 4 6 8 10 9 7 5 3 1

ISBN 0-87406-629-8

"Mother, Mother!" six-year-old George Washington called out excitedly. "Is that him? Is that my brother Lawrence?"

Mary Ball Washington looked where George was pointing. She saw a man wave from a boat on the Potomac River.

"Yes," George's mother answered proudly, "that's your brother, and just look how tall he is!"

This was a very special day for George because he had never met Lawrence. Lawrence was 20 years old. But Lawrence had been only 11 when he left for England to go to school. There were few schools for older children where George lived, in what is now called the state of Virginia. Because of that, many families sent their older children to schools in England.

George's home was on a farm called Little Hunting Creek. He lived there with three younger brothers and a sister. Little Hunting Creek farm was in the wilderness, far away from everything. George liked it there. He romped in the fields and played in the barn. There were streams with fish. In the stables, there were big, strong horses, plus ponies for George to ride.

But George thought England must be much more exciting. To George, England was a place where boys went to become gentlemen. When George was a boy—more than 250 years ago—being a gentleman was considered very important. Gentlemen worked hard at being polite, considerate of others, and well-mannered. They also did their best to dress neatly and learn about a lot of subjects.

After spending some time with Lawrence, George could tell that his brother was a gentleman. Lawrence knew about so many things, and he could talk about almost anything.

Not long after Lawrence got home, George's father, Augustine Washington, said he had an important plan to talk about.

"It's time for George to start school," Augustine Washington said to Lawrence. "There is no school at Little Hunting Creek. But if you keep up the farm here, then I can move the rest of the family to a new farm I have my eye on. It's called Ferry Farm. There's a school near it."

Ferry Farm was close to Fredericksburg, a town by the Rappahannock River. Best of all, the new farm was only a boat ride away from Little Hunting Creek! George would still be able to visit Lawrence.

Lawrence agreed that the plan was good. Before long, the family packed to leave.

After moving to Ferry Farm, George went to school with about 12 other students. Arithmetic was his favorite subject, but he also did some writing. George very much wanted to be a gentleman like Lawrence, so one time he wrote down these rules in school:

- Give not advice without being asked.
- Do not sing to yourself, nor drum your fingers or your feet.
- Cleanse not your teeth with your tablecloth.

When he wasn't doing chores or schoolwork, George visited Lawrence. He listened to the wonderful stories that Lawrence told about England. They rode horses together and explored Little Hunting Creek.

Riding beside Lawrence, who sat tall and high in the saddle, George saw more of the land than he had ever seen on his own. He came to love the gentle slope of the hillside where the creek began. He came to recognize the scuffling sound in the woods when he surprised a fox. And he came to know the smells of the wilderness—the musty odor of pine, the rich smell of rotting leaves, and the wonderful fragrance of wild flowers in bloom.

One day, when George was eight, Lawrence said that he had some news. "I am joining the Navy," he said. "England is at war with Spain and I want to help fight."

It might seem strange that Lawrence would join the English navy. But in 1740, most of the eastern United States was really part of England. England's king was in charge of the United States. In fact, the country was not even called the United States. The states were called American colonies. So when Lawrence joined the navy to fight in the war between England and Spain, he was really fighting for his own country.

George was very proud of Lawrence, but he was also afraid that Lawrence would be killed in battle. When Lawrence saw the look on George's face, he winked and said, "Don't worry about me. Just think of all the stories I'll have when I come back!"

While Lawrence was at sea, George spent his time the way most boys did—going to school and doing chores around the farm. George's father was often away on business. George was the oldest child at home and his mother really needed him to help out.

Lawrence came home when George was 11. He was full of stories about battles. Even though England had lost the war, Lawrence had been a hero. He was given a job in a small army in Virginia.

George was happy to have Lawrence home, but not long after that, their lives turned sad. One day, when George was visiting his cousins, a messenger arrived. He said that George had to go home at once. His father was very sick.

When George arrived home, Ferry Farm seemed strangely quiet. He saw his mother's sad face, and he knew that his father would never get well. In just a couple of days, George's father died.

Ferry Farm was never the same again. George's mother started to depend on his help more than ever. But she also fussed over him all the time. She always asked him if he was feeling all right. And she warned him against doing too much, because she was afraid that he would hurt himself.

One day, George's mother said she wanted to talk to him about going to England. George got very excited. He had always been told he would go to school in England like Lawrence had.

But George's mother had bad news. "George," she said, "I'm afraid that we can't manage to send you to school in England."

Tears sprang to George's eyes. "Why?" he managed to ask.

"Since your father died, we have had less money," George's mother answered. "I just can't afford to send you. I'm sorry."

George was very disappointed. He understood what his mother was saying. But he also thought that what she said was only partly true. George thought that his mother didn't want him to go because she needed his help at Ferry Farm. He also thought she would worry about him if he was so far away.

So instead of going to school in England, George did the next best thing—he spent as much time as he could with Lawrence at Little Hunting Creek. Even though Lawrence had gotten married, he always had time for George. The two brothers continued to explore, but Lawrence also taught George about farming, and how to work the land. Little Hunting Creek grew tobacco, wheat, and corn.

Best of all, Lawrence taught George how to be a gentleman. Lawrence and his wife, Anne Fairfax Washington, showed George everything—how to dance, how to talk politely, and how to dress nicely.

Anne and Lawrence also built a magnificent mansion at Little Hunting Creek and called it Mount Vernon. Lawrence told George that he could live at Mount Vernon whenever he wanted.

In his spare time at Mount Vernon, George developed new hobbies—surveying and map-making. He surveyed the land, measuring it with special tools. Then, back at Mount Vernon, he would study his measurements. From his measurements he would draw maps of Little Hunting Creek and the land around it.

One day, Lawrence and George were talking with Lord Fairfax, Anne's cousin and one of the richest men in all of the colonies. Lord Fairfax liked George, and he knew that George was good with numbers and surveying land.

"George," said Lord Fairfax, "I'd like to offer you a job—a job where you'll have an adventure every day! I'd like you to help my surveyor make maps of some of my territories in the wilderness. What do you think?"

Sixteen-year-old George didn't have to think twice. He took the job.

For 33 days, George explored the wilderness. He rode deep into the forests, making his own paths through the thick brush. He saw rattlesnakes and bears. He crossed roaring rivers and rode horseback to the tops of tall mountains. And he met Indians who showed him a special war dance in front of a roaring fire.

When George returned, Lord Fairfax was very happy with the maps that George had drawn. Before George knew it, he had a new career as a surveyor. George traveled through the wilderness, making maps of new territories. He got to know and love the land as few people did.

When George was almost 20, Lawrence got sick. He had tuberculosis, a disease that made him cough a lot. Doctors told him that a trip to a warmer place might make him feel better. Lawrence's wife needed to stay home with their new baby. So Lawrence asked George to sail with him to the Caribbean, south of Florida. The Caribbean was warm and had many islands.

George hated to leave his surveying job, but he was worried about Lawrence. The two of them made the long trip to the Caribbean. But after they arrived, George himself got very sick. He caught smallpox, a disease that caused headaches and a high fever. Months passed before George and Lawrence began to feel better. George returned to Virginia, but Lawrence decided to stay in the Caribbean a little longer.

Before long, though, Lawrence wrote to say that his health had grown worse again. After a few months, he decided to sail home. But even at home, Lawrence only got worse and worse. When he died, George was more sad than he had ever been.

After Lawrence died, George wanted more than ever to do his best. He knew that Lawrence would have wanted him to always try his hardest at everything he did.

George was only 20 years old. He had never been a soldier before, but he asked to be in the army. Soon George was made a major, just as his brother had been.

George's first task as a major was very difficult. The French were setting up forts in the Ohio River valley. This was territory that England had already claimed. George rode with six other men into the wilderness to ask the French to leave. The French said no. They said they had just as much right to the land as the British.

George was used to the wilderness, but the journey out of the valley was very hard, even for him. The weather was icy cold. The land was more rugged than he remembered. But George did not give up. He returned home with the message that the French would not go.

Arguing among the French and English got worse and worse. Finally, war was declared and George led soldiers into battle. Wearing bright red coats, George and his soldiers fought against the French and against the Indians who were helping the French. The war was called the French and Indian War.

George's soldiers marched through the deep woods. They hacked out trails as they went. One time, Indians surprised George and killed many of his soldiers. The battles that followed were bloody. Many were fought on rain-soaked fields in deep mud.

In one battle, a horse was shot out from under George. He mounted another horse, and that one was also shot out from under him. Several times, bullets came close to him. A few of them even nicked his uniform.

In the end, the war was won for England. George became a hero throughout the American colonies.

After the war, George returned to Mount Vernon. Lawrence's family had moved away, and Mount Vernon seemed very quiet. But a few years later, George married Martha Dandridge Custis. Martha was a widow with two children of her own. Soon, there were voices everywhere again. George loved and took care of his new family. He also took care of Lawrence's land just the way that Lawrence would have. To George, Mount Vernon was special. He would always call it home.

George spent 16 happy years at Mount Vernon, living the life of a country gentleman. He hunted for fox. He watched over the planting of the fields and the harvesting of crops. He gave wonderful parties where couples danced for hours.

George's peaceful life was shattered in 1775, when there was talk of another war. This one was called the Revolutionary War, or the War for Independence. Like George, most people who lived in the American colonies wanted to form their own country. They were tired of living by England's rules—rules that they felt they had no say in. The colonies formed an army. George, now 43 years old, agreed to lead the army into battle.

George knew the job wouldn't be easy. But it must have been even harder than he had imagined. After two years of

fighting, George and his army were losing.

One winter, they camped at Valley Forge, a place in what is now Pennsylvania. The weather was biting cold. The driving snow was fierce. Many of the soldiers did not have warm clothes or even shoes. There was not enough food to go around. But when George felt discouraged, he thought about Lawrence. He knew that Lawrence would have wanted the colonies to form their own country as much as he did.

It took eight years for George to lead the army to victory. But the colonists did win the war, and soon they made plans to form a new country—the United States. The day that happened was a proud day in George's life. But there was a prouder day yet to come. Representatives from each new state got together. They voted to make George the first president of the new United States. George would govern the land that he loved so dearly.

George Washington was president for eight years. Then he returned to Mount Vernon. He went back to the simple life. He tended the farm, took long walks, and spent time with his family—which now included grandchildren. For George, it was the best life possible.

One cold and wet day in December, George rode his horse all around Mount Vernon. He was 67 years old, and he became very ill. A few days later, he died.

George had lived up to his brother's dreams for him. But he had lived up to his own dreams, too. He had become a gentleman. He had fought hard for the land that he loved. And from the wilderness he had helped to create a new country. The new country was a place where people had a chance to live up to their dreams. Lawrence would have been very proud.

Important Events in George Washington's Life

1732 George Washington is born on February 22.

1738 George meets his brother Lawrence for the first time.

1743 George's father, Augustine Washington, dies.

1748 George begins his career as a surveyor.

1751 George and Lawrence go to the Caribbean when Lawrence becomes ill.

1752 Lawrence dies.

1753 George travels into the wilderness to ask the French to leave English territory in the American colonies.

1754 The French and Indian War begins.

1759 George marries Martha Dandridge Custis.

1775 George is asked to lead the colonies into battle against the British.

1777 George and his troops spend a freezing winter fighting for survival at Valley Forge.

1783 George and his armies win the Revolutionary War.

1789 George becomes the first president of the United States.

1796 George retires from the presidency and returns to Mount Vernon.

1799 George dies on December 14.